mylemarks™

HELPING KIDS ALONG THE WAY!

BIG BOOK OF FEELINGS

Z. ANDREW JATAU

FEELING WORDS

Below are the 30 feelings words that you will be learning in this book! Which ones do you know already?

Angry

Proud

Lonely

Jealous

Playful

Anxious

Stressed

Happy

Courageous

Embarrassed

Curious

Surprised

Sad

Scared

Impatient

Grateful

Frustrated

Excited

Hopeless

Exhausted

Relaxed

Grumpy

Disappointed

Irritated

Confused

Shy

Guilty

Bored

Confident

Insecure

INTRODUCTION

Big Book of Feelings is designed to help your child learn more about the different feelings that he or she may experience on a daily basis. Feelings identification is beneficial in assisting your child in better accurately expressing themselves in certain situations.

With each feeling word covered in this book, definitions are given, and short story examples are illustrated to help provide further clarification. **Similar feeling words** are listed underneath the examples as a way to assist your child in identifying like feelings. Your child will then have an opportunity to draw and write about their own experiences, allowing them to personally identify with each feeling.

Big Book of Feelings is also helpful in promoting the use of empathy. Empathy is defined as the ability to view experiences from another person's perspective. By reading each story, your child will be able to identify with the characters and how they are feeling in each circumstance. You can further explore with your child by asking them how *they* would feel if put in the same situation. They could be feeling similarly to the characters in the book, or they might be able to recognize and express an alternate emotion.

The last section in this book is the **Feelings Journal**. This journal is intended for your child to write and draw about their experiences with feelings that they learn from this workbook. It is beneficial to talk to your child about the difference between *pleasant* and *unpleasant* feelings.

Pleasant feelings are ones that we enjoy experiencing and hope will continue to happen.

Unpleasant feelings are ones that we would rather not go through again.

With unpleasant feelings such as anger, sadness, or anxiety, your child will have a record of how they dealt with it in the past and can recognize whether they need to cope differently in the future.

BIG

BOOK

OF

FEELINGS

ANGRY

Angry is how you feel when you don't get your way or when someone does something that you really don't like.

Alyssa has been showing off her new shoes to all of her friends. Her classmate, Debbie, is tired of hearing her talk about her shoes all day. When the class goes outside for recess, Debbie bumps into Alyssa and steps on her shoe on purpose! Alyssa's shoe is now dirty! Alyssa is feeling **angry**.

SIMILAR FEELING WORDS: MAD, UPSET

Write about a time when you felt <u>angry</u>!

_____

_____

_____

_____

Draw a picture of a time when you felt <u>angry</u>!

ANXIOUS

Anxious is how you feel when something is about to happen, but you're not sure if it'll be good or bad.

Tony is on the bus home from school. His friend is trying to talk to him, but he's having a hard time paying attention. Instead, Tony is thinking about what might happen when he gets home. He got in trouble at school today because he kept making funny noises in class while the teacher was talking. Tony is not sure if his teacher called home and told his parents. Tony is feeling **anxious**.

SIMILAR FEELING WORDS: NERVOUS, UNEASY

Write about a time when you felt <u>anxious</u>!

_____

_____

_____

_____

_____

Draw a picture of a time when you felt <u>anxious</u>!

BORED

Bored is how you feel when you don't have anything to do, or you're not doing anything fun in the moment.

Truman is at the store with his mom. After 30 minutes, Truman asks, "Is it time to go yet?" His mom tells him that it will only be a few more minutes. As they are about to leave, Truman's mom sees their neighbor, and they end up talking for another 45 minutes! Truman just sits outside on the bench with nothing to do. Truman is feeling **bored**.

SIMILAR FEELINGS WORDS: UNINTERESTED, DULL

Write about a time when you felt <u>bored</u>!

_____

_____

_____

_____

_____

Draw a picture of a time when you felt <u>bored</u>!

CONFIDENT

Confident is how you feel when you believe that you can accomplish something and that you will be good at it.

Sandra has been working on her volcano science project for the past two weeks. She has been going to the library every day and has learned everything she needs to know about volcanoes. Sandra will enter her project into the school science fair tomorrow, and she believes that she will be able to win the first-place ribbon! Sandra is feeling **confident**.

SIMILAR FEELING WORDS: CERTAIN, ENCOURAGED

Write about a time when you felt <u>confident</u>!

_____

_____

_____

_____

_____

Draw a picture of a time when you felt <u>confident</u>!

CONFUSED

Confused is how you feel when something doesn't make sense to you.

Mason is sitting in class, ready to take his spelling quiz. He studied really hard for it so that he can get a good grade. The teacher walks around and places the quiz on everyone's desk. Mason looks down at the paper and sees that it is a math quiz! Oh, no! Mason thought that the math quiz was supposed to be next week. Mason is feeling **confused.**

SIMILAR FEELING WORDS: PUZZLED, LOST

Write about a time when you felt <u>confused</u>!

_____

_____

_____

_____

_____

Draw a picture of a time when you felt <u>confused</u>!

COURAGEOUS

Courageous is how you feel when you are willing to face something that makes you afraid.

Clara is at her swim lessons. It is the last day, and the instructor wants everyone to practice jumping off of the diving board. The instructor asks, "Who would like to go first today?" Clara sees that no one else is raising their hand. Even though she's afraid, she decides to go ahead and give it a try. She says, "I'll go first!" Clara is feeling **courageous**.

SIMILAR FEELING WORDS: BRAVE, BOLD

Write about a time when you felt <u>courageous</u>!

_____

_____

_____

_____

_____

Draw a picture of a time when you felt <u>courageous</u>!

CURIOUS

Curious is how you feel when you want to ask questions because you really want to know or learn something.

Evan is at a magic show with his family. The magician calls Evan up to the stage so that he can see the next trick up close. The magician places a carrot on the table next to him. He waves his wand over the carrot and says, "Abracadabra!" The carrot turns into a bunny rabbit! Evan asks, "How did you do that?!" Evan is feeling **curious**.

SIMILAR FEELING WORDS: INTRIGUED, INTERESTED

Write about a time when you felt <u>curious</u>!

_____

_____

_____

_____

_____

Draw a picture of a time when you felt <u>curious</u>!

DISAPPOINTED

Disappointed is how you feel when you really want something to happen, but it doesn't.

Austin is opening gifts on Christmas morning. The only thing he really wants this year is a new skateboard! All he has received so far from his family is clothes. His dad hands him one last gift to open. Austin knows for sure that this will be a skateboard! Instead, when he opens the gift, he sees that it's a new pair of shoes. Austin is feeling **disappointed**.

SIMILAR FEELING WORDS: LET DOWN, SADDENED

Write about a time when you felt <u>disappointed</u>!

_____

_____

_____

_____

_____

Draw a picture of a time when you felt <u>disappointed</u>!

EMBARRASSED

Embarrassed is how you feel when something happens that makes you uncomfortable or that other people might laugh at you about.

Parker is at the restaurant with his family. He piles his plate full of spaghetti and begins walking back to the table. Parker isn't paying attention and ends up tripping. He falls on the ground, and his face lands in his food. He has spaghetti and sauce all over him! Everyone in the restaurant is looking at him. Parker is feeling **embarrassed**.

SIMILAR FEELING WORDS: ASHAMED, HUMILIATED

Write about a time when you felt <u>embarrassed</u>!

_____

_____

_____

_____

_____

Draw a picture of a time when you felt <u>embarrassed</u>!

EXCITED

Excited is how you feel when you have a lot of energy because you are really looking forward to something that will happen.

Sydney can't wait for the bell to ring! There are 10 minutes left in class, and it is the last day of school. After school, her parents will be picking her up, and they will be going to the beach for a family vacation. This will be her first time ever going to the beach! Sydney is ready to rush out to the car as soon as school is over. Sydney is feeling **excited**.

SIMILAR FEELING WORDS: THRILLED, ENTHUSIASTIC

Write about a time when you felt <u>excited</u>!

_____

_____

_____

_____

_____

Draw a picture of a time when you felt <u>excited</u>!

EXHAUSTED

Exhausted is how you feel when you are very tired and feel like you don't have any energy left.

Asher just got back from spending the night at his friend's house. As soon as he gets home, he has to go to his soccer game. After the game, he goes to another friend's birthday party. Once he gets home from the party, his mom makes him do all of the chores that he didn't do yesterday. Asher has had a very busy day! He is feeling **exhausted**.

SIMILAR FEELING WORDS: BEAT, DRAINED

Write about a time when you felt <u>exhausted</u>!

_____

_____

_____

_____

_____

Draw a picture of a time when you felt <u>exhausted</u>!

FRUSTRATED

Frustrated is how you feel when something is not going the way that you want it to.

Lillian just got a new train set for her birthday. She spends the whole day in her room putting it together. She's ready to take it downstairs to show it to everyone, but when she picks it up, it falls apart. Lillian doesn't know what could be wrong. She keeps trying to fix it, but it's still not working! Lillian is feeling **frustrated**.

SIMILAR FEELING WORDS: AGGRAVATED, BOTHERED

Write about a time when you felt <u>frustrated</u>!

_____

_____

_____

_____

_____

Draw a picture of a time when you felt <u>frustrated</u>!

GRATEFUL

Grateful is how you feel when you want to say "thanks!" to someone for something nice that they did for you.

Janice is in a rush to get to class before the bell rings. As she is walking, she accidentally drops all of her books and papers on the ground. Kenny sees this happen, and he stops and helps Janice pick up all of her things. Janice is glad that Kenny was there to help her when she needed it. Janice is feeling **grateful**.

SIMILAR FEELING WORDS: THANKFUL, APPRECIATIVE

Write about a time when you felt <u>grateful</u>!

_____

_____

_____

_____

_____

Draw a picture of a time when you felt <u>grateful</u>!

GRUMPY

Grumpy is how you feel when you are in a bad mood for some reason and are not being very nice to others.

Chucky wakes up to the sound of the loud T.V. in the other room. He is really tired because he didn't fall asleep until very late last night. Chucky goes to the living room and sees that his little sister is watching cartoons. "Turn the volume down!" he yells. Chucky is not usually mean to her, but he's just in a bad mood today. Chucky is feeling **grumpy**.

SIMILAR FEELING WORDS: GROUCHY, CRANKY

Write about a time when you felt <u>grumpy</u>!

_____

_____

_____

_____

_____

Draw a picture of a time when you felt <u>grumpy</u>!

GUILTY

Guilty is how you feel when you do something that you shouldn't have and you want to do something to make it better.

Amy and her sister, Francine, are throwing a ball across the living room. Amy throws it too high, and it goes over Francine's head and breaks the lamp. Their mom runs into the living room and says, "Francine, what did you do? Go to your room!" Francine goes to her room and has to stay up there for a whole hour! Amy knows that she should have told her mom that it wasn't Francine's fault. Amy is feeling **guilty**.

SIMILAR FEELING WORDS: SHAMEFUL, REMORSEFUL

Write about a time when you felt <u>guilty</u>!

_____

_____

_____

_____

_____

Draw a picture of a time when you felt <u>guilty</u>!

HAPPY

Happy is how you feel when you are really enjoying something that is happening and it makes you want to smile.

Simon is walking to school wearing his brand-new shoes. "Hey Simon, nice shoes!" his neighbor says to him when he walks by. Simon smiles and says, "Thanks!" When Simon gets to school, he finds out that he got an A+ on his reading test. At lunch, the cafeteria is serving pizza and fries. This is his favorite meal! He is having a really good day. Simon is feeling **happy**.

SIMILAR FEELINGS WORDS: CONTENT, CHEERFUL

Write about a time when you felt <u>happy</u>!

_____

_____

_____

_____

_____

Draw a picture of a time when you felt <u>happy</u>!

HOPELESS

Hopeless is how you feel when you believe that something is not going to change no matter what you do about it.

Gabby just got a new video game. She has been playing it for the last few hours trying to beat all of the levels. She is having a hard time making it past the last round. She keeps trying, but no matter what she does, she always ends up losing. She tries again the next day, but she just can't beat the level! She's ready to give up. Gabby is feeling **hopeless**.

SIMILAR FEELING WORDS: HELPLESS, DOWNHEARTED

Write about a time when you felt <u>hopeless</u>!

_____

_____

_____

_____

_____

Draw a picture of a time when you felt <u>hopeless</u>!

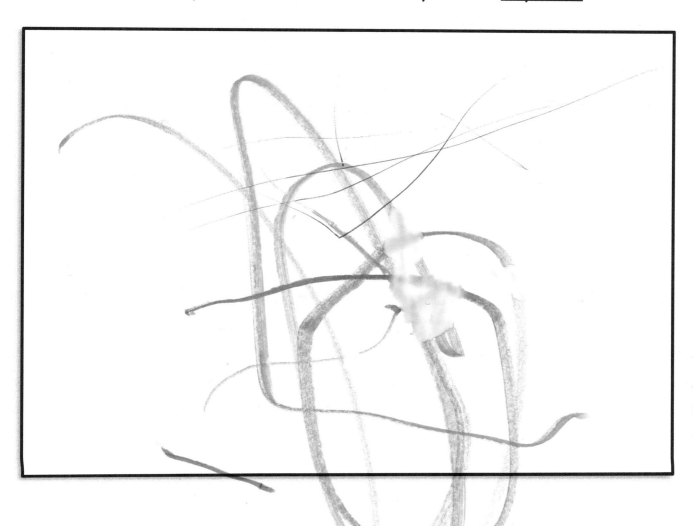

IMPATIENT

Impatient is how you feel when you want something to happen quicker because you don't feel like waiting.

Saul's dad drops him off at the movie theater. Saul's friends are already inside and are saving him a seat. He gets into the line to buy his ticket. Saul needs to hurry because the movie is starting right now! The people in front of him are taking too long, so he decides to jump in front of everyone so that he can get his ticket quicker! Saul is feeling **impatient**.

SIMILAR FEELING WORDS: EAGER, HURRIED

Write about a time when you felt <u>impatient</u>!

_____

_____

_____

_____

_____

Draw a picture of a time when you felt <u>impatient</u>!

INSECURE

Insecure is how you feel when you don't believe in yourself or when you don't think you're as good as other people.

Sage's friends ask her if she wants to go roller skating with them. She has only been skating once before, and she wasn't very good at it. She fell down a lot! All of her friends can skate really well. They can even skate backwards! She decides to go with them, but she doesn't think that she's going to do well. Sage is feeling **insecure**.

SIMILAR FEELING WORDS: UNCONFIDENT, DOUBTFUL

Write about a time when you felt <u>insecure</u>!

_____

_____

_____

_____

_____

Draw a picture of a time when you felt <u>insecure</u>!

IRRITATED

Irritated is how you feel when something or someone keeps bugging you and puts you in a bad mood.

Gale is teaching her little brother how to tie his shoes. As she is helping him, her dog, Pip, grabs his shoe and takes off running! Gale chases Pip around the neighborhood and gets the shoe back. She starts helping her brother again, but Pip keeps on taking the shoe and running off. Gale is feeling **irritated**.

SIMILAR FEELING WORDS: ANGRY, ANNOYED

Write about a time when you felt <u>irritated</u>!

_____

_____

_____

_____

_____

Draw a picture of a time when you felt <u>irritated</u>!

JEALOUS

Jealous is how you feel when someone else has something that you really wished was yours.

Trevor is walking home from the park. His friend, Jeff, pulls up on his new bike. "Hey Trevor, check out my bike! It's a Mountain Bike LX2000 Extreme," he says. It's the same bike Trevor has been asking his parents to buy him for the last few months! He really wants a new bike, but he knows his parents won't buy him one. Trevor is feeling **jealous**.

SIMILAR FEELING WORDS: ENVIOUS, BITTER

Write about a time when you felt <u>jealous</u>!

_____

_____

_____

_____

_____

Draw a picture of a time when you felt <u>jealous</u>!

LONELY

Lonely is how you feel when you are by yourself, but you want to be around others or be included in what they are doing.

Olivia is the last one to finish her quiz in class. Everyone else is already outside on the playground. When she finally gets outside, she sees that she's too late. Her friends have already picked teams for the kickball game. She is unable to play and has to sit on the bench by herself and watch. Olivia is feeling **lonely.**

SIMILAR FEELING WORDS: ISOLATED, SECLUDED

Write about a time when you felt <u>lonely</u>!

_____

_____

_____

_____

_____

Draw a picture of a time when you felt <u>lonely</u>!

PLAYFUL

Playful is how you feel when you are in a good mood and you feel like joking around and having fun.

Wes is sitting at the table eating breakfast. He grabs his fork and spoon and starts pretending that they are airplanes landing in his mouth! "Coming in for a landing! Open wide!" he says as he takes a big bite from his spoon. Wes grabs his fork and says, "All passengers prepare for landing!" He is having fun joking around. Wes is feeling **playful**.

SIMILAR FEELING WORDS: LIVELY, GOOD-HUMORED

Write about a time when you felt <u>playful</u>!

_____

_____

_____

_____

Draw a picture of a time when you felt <u>playful</u>!

PROUD

Proud is how you feel when you've put in a lot of time and effort to accomplish something.

Luke has been studying for the spelling bee all week. It is the day of the spelling bee, and it's down to Luke and another classmate. If Luke spells the next word correctly, he wins! The teacher asks Luke to spell "camp". Luke thinks for a second and then spells out, "c-a-m-p". The teacher says, "Correct!" Luke wins the spelling bee and is feeling **proud!**

SIMILAR FEELING WORDS: HONORED, FULFILLED

Write about a time when you felt <u>proud</u>!

_____

_____

_____

_____

Draw a picture of a time when you felt <u>proud</u>!

RELAXED

Relaxed is how you feel when you have nothing to worry about.

Kyra just got home from school. Her dad says, "After softball practice today, make sure to do your homework and finish all your chores." Kyra still has time before practice, so she does all her chores and is even able to finish her homework assignment. When she gets home after practice, she knows that everything she needed to do is already completed. Kyra is feeling **relaxed**.

SIMILAR FEELING WORDS: CALM, COMFORTABLE

Write about a time when you felt <u>relaxed</u>!

_____

_____

_____

_____

Draw a picture of a time when you felt <u>relaxed</u>!

SAD

Sad is how you feel when it is really hard to smile because something bad has happened.

Chaz is walking his dog, Scoop, around the block. He stops by his friend's house to visit. There are no dogs allowed in the house, so he ties Scoop's leash to the tree out front. Chaz goes inside to play for a few minutes. When it's time to leave, he goes to the tree to get Scoop, but he is gone! He must have run away! Chaz is feeling **sad**.

SIMILAR FEELING WORDS: GLOOMY, UNHAPPY

Write about a time when you felt <u>sad</u>!

_____

_____

_____

_____

_____

Draw a picture of a time when you felt <u>sad</u>!

SCARED

Scared is how you feel when you don't want to do something because you think it will put you in danger.

Stella is at the park with her friends. Her friends want to go on a ride called *Ghost House*. On this ride, ghosts hide in the dark and jump out at you when you're not looking! Stella thinks that the ghosts might try to take her away! Her friends are trying to get her to come on the ride with them, but she doesn't think she can do it. She really wants to turn back around. Stella is feeling **scared**.

SIMILAR FEELING WORDS: TERRIFIED, FEARFUL

Write about a time when you felt <u>scared</u>!

_____

_____

_____

_____

_____

Draw a picture of a time when you felt <u>scared</u>!

SHY

Shy is how you feel when you are around other people, but you are afraid to say anything to them.

Ida's family just moved into the neighborhood last week, and it is her first day of school today. Ida doesn't raise her hand or talk to anyone the whole time that she is sitting in class. At recess, she really wants to go and play with the other kids, but she doesn't know if they will like her or not. Ida is not sure what to say to them. Ida is feeling **shy**.

SIMILAR FEELING WORDS: CAUTIOUS, WARY

Write about a time when you felt <u>shy</u>!

_____

_____

_____

_____

Draw a picture of a time when you felt <u>shy</u>!

STRESSED

Stressed is how you feel when you have a lot of important things going on, or you have big decisions to make.

Samantha sure has a lot going on! She has to write a paper for class that is due tomorrow. She is not sure if she will be able to get it done because she has basketball practice *and* her piano recital right after school today! She won't be home until very late tonight. Samantha is not sure if she'll be able to complete her paper by tomorrow. Samantha is feeling **stressed**.

SIMILAR FEELING WORDS: FRAZZLED, HASSLED

Write about a time when you felt <u>stressed</u>!

_____

_____

_____

_____

_____

Draw a picture of a time when you felt <u>stressed</u>!

SURPRISED

Surprised is how you feel when you had no idea that what just happened was going to happen.

Patricia's birthday is today! As she is eating breakfast with her family, no one mentions anything to her. She thinks that maybe they all forgot about her birthday! As Patricia is getting in the car to go to school, her family walks out of the house holding presents for her. "Happy Birthday, Patricia!" they all yell. She wasn't expecting this at all! Patricia is feeling **surprised**.

SIMILAR FEELING WORDS: STARTLED, AMAZED

Write about a time when you felt <u>surprised</u>!

_____

_____

_____

_____

_____

Draw a picture of a time when you felt <u>surprised</u>!

ACTIVITY

Cory's kite blows away with the wind when he is flying it outside.

CIRCLE THE WORDS THAT DESCRIBE HOW CORY MIGHT BE FEELING!

angry	confused	lonely	disappointed	stressed
jealous	playful	anxious	embarrassed	scared
courageous	curious	sad	surprised	happy
excited	exhausted	hopeless	relaxed	grateful
irritated	grumpy	shy	guilty	frustrated
bored	proud	confident	impatient	insecure

Dennis learns how to play a new song on the piano.

CIRCLE THE WORDS THAT DESCRIBE HOW DENNIS MIGHT BE FEELING!

angry	confused	lonely	disappointed	stressed
jealous	playful	anxious	embarrassed	scared
courageous	curious	sad	surprised	happy
excited	exhausted	hopeless	relaxed	grateful
irritated	grumpy	shy	guilty	frustrated
bored	proud	confident	impatient	insecure

Coretta gets a good grade on her test. She studied for it all week!

CIRCLE THE WORDS THAT DESCRIBE HOW CORETTA MIGHT BE FEELING!

angry	confused	lonely	disappointed	stressed
jealous	playful	anxious	embarrassed	scared
courageous	curious	sad	surprised	happy
excited	exhausted	hopeless	relaxed	grateful
irritated	grumpy	shy	guilty	frustrated
bored	proud	confident	impatient	insecure

Otis drops his cup of milk in the living room, and it spills all over the floor.

CIRCLE THE WORDS THAT DESCRIBE HOW OTIS MIGHT BE FEELING!

angry	confused	lonely	disappointed	stressed
jealous	playful	anxious	embarrassed	scared
courageous	curious	sad	surprised	happy
excited	exhausted	hopeless	relaxed	grateful
irritated	grumpy	shy	guilty	frustrated
bored	proud	confident	impatient	insecure

Phoebe's dad makes pizza for dinner. This is her favorite meal!

CIRCLE THE WORDS THAT DESCRIBE HOW PHOEBE MIGHT BE FEELING!

angry	confused	lonely	disappointed	stressed
jealous	playful	anxious	embarrassed	scared
courageous	curious	sad	surprised	happy
excited	exhausted	hopeless	relaxed	grateful
irritated	grumpy	shy	guilty	frustrated
bored	proud	confident	impatient	insecure

Veronica hurts her knee. Aaron laughs at her because she is crying.

CIRCLE THE WORDS THAT DESCRIBE HOW VERONICA MIGHT BE FEELING!

angry	confused	lonely	disappointed	stressed
jealous	playful	anxious	embarrassed	scared
courageous	curious	sad	surprised	happy
excited	exhausted	hopeless	relaxed	grateful
irritated	grumpy	shy	guilty	frustrated
bored	proud	confident	impatient	insecure

Wendy can't find her homework, and she's about to miss the bus.

CIRCLE THE WORDS THAT DESCRIBE HOW WENDY MIGHT BE FEELING!

angry	confused	lonely	disappointed	stressed
jealous	playful	anxious	embarrassed	scared
courageous	curious	sad	surprised	happy
excited	exhausted	hopeless	relaxed	grateful
irritated	grumpy	shy	guilty	frustrated
bored	proud	confident	impatient	insecure

Lance is looking forward to playing the new video game he just got.

CIRCLE THE WORDS THAT DESCRIBE HOW LANCE MIGHT BE FEELING!

angry	confused	lonely	disappointed	stressed
jealous	playful	anxious	embarrassed	scared
courageous	curious	sad	surprised	happy
excited	exhausted	hopeless	relaxed	grateful
irritated	grumpy	shy	guilty	frustrated
bored	proud	confident	impatient	insecure

CIRCLE ALL THE FEELING WORDS THAT YOU'VE LEARNED!

Words can be frontwards, backwards, or diagonal

```
K  V  S  C  S  U  O  E  G  A  R  U  O  C  F  L  H
A  E  M  B  A  R  R  A  S  S  E  D  P  O  S  U  Z
R  X  H  O  G  U  I  L  T  Y  Z  I  L  N  G  F  C
E  H  J  R  D  E  S  S  E  R  T  S  A  F  S  E  U
D  A  F  E  U  N  H  C  G  G  R  A  Y  I  R  T  R
E  U  B  D  O  Y  M  A  F  N  E  P  F  D  X  A  I
T  S  U  L  R  T  C  R  D  A  S  P  U  E  D  R  O
A  T  H  O  P  E  L  E  S  S  B  O  L  N  E  G  U
R  E  F  G  L  O  X  D  Q  Y  M  I  X  T  S  J  S
T  D  A  S  N  C  Y  P  P  A  H  N  P  E  U  E  J
S  N  M  E  I  K  O  M  K  R  S  T  A  D  F  A  M
U  B  L  T  G  H  U  E  B  A  S  E  I  S  N  L  A
R  Y  E  L  K  R  E  L  A  X  E  D  N  G  O  O  R
F  D  V  X  G  I  N  S  E  C  U  R  E  R  C  U  I
I  R  R  I  T  A  T  E  D  Y  N  S  C  A  M  S  E
A  N  X  I  O  U  S  I  M  P  A  T  I  E  N  T  K
P  D  G  F  S  U  R  P  R  I  S  E  D  U  P  V  R
```

ANGRY	EXCITED	HOPELESS	RELAXED
ANXIOUS	EXHAUSTED	IMPATIENT	SAD
BORED	FRUSTRATED	INSECURE	SCARED
CONFIDENT	GRATEFUL	IRRITATED	SHY
CONFUSED	GRUMPY	JEALOUS	STRESSED
CURIOUS	GUILTY	LONELY	SURPRISED
DISAPPOINTED	HAPPY	PLAYFUL	
EMBARRASSED	COURAGEOUS	PROUD	

MY FEELINGS JOURNAL

FEELING WORD: _____

What happened to make you feel this way? _____

_____

DRAW A PICTURE OF WHAT HAPPENED!

Was this a pleasant feeling?   **YES**   **NO**

If it was a pleasant feeling, that's great! If it was an unpleasant feeling, how did you handle it?

_____

_____

How could you have handled it better?

_____

_____

FEELING WORD: _____

What happened to make you feel this way? _____

_____

DRAW A PICTURE OF WHAT HAPPENED!

```
┌──────────────────────────────────────────────┐
│                                                │
│                                                │
│                                                │
│                                                │
│                                                │
│                                                │
│                                                │
│                                                │
│                                                │
│                                                │
└──────────────────────────────────────────────┘
```

Was this a pleasant feeling?   **YES**   **NO**

If it was a pleasant feeling, that's great! If it was an unpleasant feeling, how did you handle it?

_____

_____

How could you have handled it better?

_____

_____

FEELING WORD: _____

What happened to make you feel this way? _____

_____

DRAW A PICTURE OF WHAT HAPPENED!

Was this a pleasant feeling?   **YES**   **NO**

If it was a pleasant feeling, that's great! If it was an unpleasant feeling, how did you handle it?

_____

_____

How could you have handled it better?

_____

_____

FEELING WORD: _____

What happened to make you feel this way? _____

_____

DRAW A PICTURE OF WHAT HAPPENED!

Was this a pleasant feeling?   **YES**   **NO**

If it was a pleasant feeling, that's great! If it was an unpleasant feeling, how did you handle it?

_____

_____

How could you have handled it better?

_____

_____

FEELING WORD: _____

What happened to make you feel this way? _____

_____

DRAW A PICTURE OF WHAT HAPPENED!

Was this a pleasant feeling?   **YES**   **NO**

If it was a pleasant feeling, that's great! If it was an unpleasant feeling, how did you handle it?

_____

_____

How could you have handled it better?

_____

_____

FEELING WORD: _____

What happened to make you feel this way? _____

_____

DRAW A PICTURE OF WHAT HAPPENED!

Was this a pleasant feeling?   **YES**   **NO**

If it was a pleasant feeling, that's great! If it was an unpleasant feeling, how did you handle it?

_____

_____

How could you have handled it better?

_____

_____

FEELING WORD: _____

What happened to make you feel this way? _____

_____

DRAW A PICTURE OF WHAT HAPPENED!

Was this a pleasant feeling?   **YES**   **NO**

If it was a pleasant feeling, that's great! If it was an unpleasant feeling, how did you handle it?

_____

_____

How could you have handled it better?

_____

_____

FEELING WORD: _____

What happened to make you feel this way? _____

_____

DRAW A PICTURE OF WHAT HAPPENED!

┌───┐
│   │
│   │
│   │
│   │
│   │
│   │
│   │
│   │
│   │
└───┘

Was this a pleasant feeling?   **YES**   **NO**

If it was a pleasant feeling, that's great! If it was an unpleasant feeling, how did you handle it?

_____

_____

How could you have handled it better?

_____

_____

FEELING WORD: _____

What happened to make you feel this way? _____

_____

DRAW A PICTURE OF WHAT HAPPENED!

Was this a pleasant feeling?   **YES**   **NO**

If it was a pleasant feeling, that's great! If it was an unpleasant feeling, how did you handle it?

_____

_____

How could you have handled it better?

_____

_____

FEELING WORD: _____

What happened to make you feel this way? _____

_____

DRAW A PICTURE OF WHAT HAPPENED!

Was this a pleasant feeling?   **YES**   **NO**

If it was a pleasant feeling, that's great! If it was an unpleasant feeling, how did you handle it?

_____

_____

How could you have handled it better?

_____

_____

FEELING WORD: _____

What happened to make you feel this way? _____

_____

DRAW A PICTURE OF WHAT HAPPENED!

Was this a pleasant feeling? **YES** **NO**

If it was a pleasant feeling, that's great! If it was an unpleasant feeling, how did you handle it?

_____

_____

How could you have handled it better?

_____

_____

FEELING WORD: _____

What happened to make you feel this way? _____

_____

DRAW A PICTURE OF WHAT HAPPENED!

```
┌─────────────────────────────────────────────┐
│                                             │
│                                             │
│                                             │
│                                             │
│                                             │
│                                             │
│                                             │
│                                             │
│                                             │
│                                             │
└─────────────────────────────────────────────┘
```

Was this a pleasant feeling?   **YES**   **NO**

If it was a pleasant feeling, that's great! If it was an unpleasant feeling, how did you handle it?

_____

_____

How could you have handled it better?

_____

_____

FEELING WORD: _____

What happened to make you feel this way? _____

_____

DRAW A PICTURE OF WHAT HAPPENED!

Was this a pleasant feeling?   **YES**   **NO**

If it was a pleasant feeling, that's great! If it was an unpleasant feeling, how did you handle it?

_____

_____

How could you have handled it better?

_____

_____

FEELING WORD: _____

What happened to make you feel this way? _____

_____

DRAW A PICTURE OF WHAT HAPPENED!

Was this a pleasant feeling?   **YES**   **NO**

If it was a pleasant feeling, that's great! If it was an unpleasant feeling, how did you handle it?

_____

_____

How could you have handled it better?

_____

_____

FEELING WORD: _____

What happened to make you feel this way? _____

_____

DRAW A PICTURE OF WHAT HAPPENED!

Was this a pleasant feeling?   **YES**   **NO**

If it was a pleasant feeling, that's great! If it was an unpleasant feeling, how did you handle it?

_____

_____

How could you have handled it better?

_____

_____

FEELING WORD: _____

What happened to make you feel this way? _____

_____

DRAW A PICTURE OF WHAT HAPPENED!

[ ]

Was this a pleasant feeling?   **YES**   **NO**

If it was a pleasant feeling, that's great! If it was an unpleasant feeling, how did you handle it?

_____

_____

How could you have handled it better?

_____

_____

FEELING WORD: _____

What happened to make you feel this way? _____

_____

DRAW A PICTURE OF WHAT HAPPENED!

Was this a pleasant feeling?   **YES**   **NO**

If it was a pleasant feeling, that's great! If it was an unpleasant feeling, how did you handle it?

_____

_____

How could you have handled it better?

_____

_____

FEELING WORD: _____

What happened to make you feel this way? _____

_____

DRAW A PICTURE OF WHAT HAPPENED!

┌───┐
│   │
│   │
│   │
│   │
│   │
│   │
│   │
│   │
│   │
│   │
└───┘

Was this a pleasant feeling?   **YES**   **NO**

If it was a pleasant feeling, that's great! If it was an unpleasant feeling, how did you handle it?

_____

_____

How could you have handled it better?

_____

_____

FEELING WORD: _____

What happened to make you feel this way? _____

_____

DRAW A PICTURE OF WHAT HAPPENED!

Was this a pleasant feeling?　　**YES**　　　　　　**NO**

If it was a pleasant feeling, that's great! If it was an unpleasant feeling, how did you handle it?

_____

_____

How could you have handled it better?

_____

_____

FEELING WORD: _____

What happened to make you feel this way? _____

_____

DRAW A PICTURE OF WHAT HAPPENED!

Was this a pleasant feeling?   **YES**   **NO**

If it was a pleasant feeling, that's great! If it was an unpleasant feeling, how did you handle it?

_____

_____

How could you have handled it better?

_____

_____

ABOUT THE AUTHOR

Z. Andrew Jatau, MS, has served diverse populations in his roles as a case manager, professional counselor, and adjunct professor. He has developed programs and presentations focused on helping children, teens, and young adults develop socially and emotionally. He is the founder and CEO of Mylemarks LLC.

FOR MORE HELPFUL SOCIAL-EMOTIONAL RESOURCES AND TOOLS, VISIT WWW.MYLEMARKS.COM!

CPSIA information can be obtained
at www.ICGtesting.com
Printed in the USA
BVHW010321131220
595588BV00035B/752